# Jewel of the Missions
# San Juan Capistrano

# Jewel of the Missions
# San Juan Capistrano

by Lorna Collins

Featuring the art of

Robert L. Schwenck

Cover Design: Larry K. Collins

ISBN: 6652556

ISBN-13: 978-1539588559

ASIN: B01MCUWGLJ

# CONTENTS

# Dedication

~Dedicated to the Historical Society of San Juan Capistrano,
which preserves the history of the town for generations to come~

# In the Beginning

During the mid-eighteenth century, Spain was a major world power. The government dispatched Jesuits to Baja California to found missions in order to convert the natives to the Roman Catholic religion. They were also put in charge of the soldiers who lived at the forts and presidios.

By June 1767, the Spanish government felt the Jesuits had become too powerful, so King Carlos transferred the existing Baja missions into the control of the Franciscans. The order was given authority over the day-to-day activities of the missions, but not the soldiers.

The Spanish government then decided to expand their influence into Alta California (now Southern California). Franciscan Father Junipero Serra (now St. Junipero Serra) was appointed to found the first mission in Alta California.

The expedition was split into groups, one to go by land and one by sea. Three ships, *San Carlos*, *San Jose*, and *San Antonio,* sailed in early 1769 from Baja, and two parties of soldiers and priests traveled overland. The difficult trip by land took its toll, and many men died. The ships did not fare much better. The *San Jose* was lost at sea with no survivors. Most missions were located near the coast because the mountain ranges and deserts in Alta California made travel difficult, while the coast allowed easier access.

Father Serra founded Mission San Diego de Alcala in 1769 and established nine missions before his death and burial at Mission San Carlos in modern Carmel in 1784. Eventually, twenty-one missions were built between 1769 and 1823 in a chain that stretched from San Diego to north of San Francisco.

Mission San Juan Capistrano was number seven of the missions founded by Father Serra.

Old Entrance
20x24 oil on canvas

Father Serra Old Mission
11x14 oil on canvas

# Founding San Juan Capistrano

Father Juan Crespí, a member of the 1769 Portolà expedition, arrived in the area of the current mission on July 23 and wrote a report about the area.

In 1775, Spain authorized the establishment of a mission between San Diego and Los Angeles. The area already bore the name of the patron saint of judges and the military, San Juan Capistrano. A wooden cross was erected to mark the spot, and two bronze bells were suspended from the branch of a nearby tree. Father Fermín Lasuén of Mission San Carlos Borromeo de Carmelo consecrated the ground on October 30, 1775.

On November 1, 1776, Father Serra and missionaries Pablo Mugártegui and Gregorio Amurrío officially founded Mission San Juan Capistrano as the seventh of the Alta California Missions. The original location is unknown, but it is believed to have been closer to the coast than its current site.

In 1778, two years after the mission's founding, it was moved to its present location. A small adobe chapel was built, but it was soon replaced by the Serra Chapel in 1782. This is the only remaining church in which Father Junipero Serra conducted Mass.

Light on Arches
16x20 oil on canvas

Mission Corner
16x20 oil on canvas

# St. Giovanni da Capistrano

Mission San Juan Capistrano was named for the patron saint of jurists and military chaplains, St. Giovanni da Capistrano (John of Capistrano). He was born in Italy in 1386.

During his early adulthood, he lived a secular life. In 1416, he became a magistrate and then the governor over Perugia. A few years later, when war broke out, he was assigned as ambassador of peace to Malatesta. However, when he arrived, he was thrown in prison. There he began to concentrate on spiritual matters. Eventually, he surrendered his life to serve God. He joined the Franciscan Order and studied theology and preaching.

After he became a priest, he traveled throughout Europe and Russia, preaching forgiveness and penance to large crowds. People stopped their activities in order to hear him. The pope and other Catholic administrators sent him all over Europe to continue spreading his positive message.

In Frankfurt, Germany in 1454, he provided insight into the upcoming war with the Turks. John was present at the battle of Belgrade and led the left wing of the Christian army against the Turks. Soon afterward, John contracted the bubonic plague and died on October 23, 1456. He was beatified in 1694, and canonized as a saint in 1724.

# The Great Stone Church

In 1797, construction began on the Great Stone Church. The small adobe chapel, in use for over ten years (now known as Serra Chapel), could not hold all of the Native Americans who lived at the mission.

Everyone in the community participated in the construction, including the women and children. Although they could not lift the two-hundred-pound stone blocks, they gathered small stones and gravel for the mortar to hold the blocks together. Over the next nine years, the entire community worked to build the church. In 1806, the structure was complete, and a grand fiesta celebrated the occasion.

Only six years later, on December 8, 1812, during the early morning Mass, a large earthquake struck.

The bell tower swayed and collapsed on the center of the church, blocking escape for those inside. The large stones fell upon forty people as they tried to exit. They were buried alive. Several others followed the priest out the priests' door at the front of the building and survived.

After the disaster, no attempt to rebuild was successful. The ruins remained as a memorial to those lost in the collapse of the church.

Over the years, the ruins of the church deteriorated. In 2002, the prestigious World Monuments Fund placed The Great Stone Church on its List of 100 Most Endangered Sites. A series of seismic reinforcements of the ruins were completed in 2004 at a cost of $7.5 million. Many visitors, including schoolchildren, visit the mission each year.

Deep Shadows Old Stone Church
16x20 oil on canvas

Old Sanctuary from Across the Street
8x10 oil on canvas

# The Mission Period

After its founding, the mission grew steadily. By 1797, the population exceeded 1000 neophytes (local natives). The highest recorded population was 1,361, in 1812.

In 1783 (the first year with detailed records) the mission had 430 cattle, 305 sheep, 830 goats, forty pigs, thirty-two horses, and one mule, a total of 1,648 animals. In 1819 (the peak year), the mission had over 31,000 animals, including 14,000 cattle and 16,000 sheep.

Production of crops also increased. Between 1783 and 1831, San Juan Capistrano harvested 234,879 bushels of wheat, barley, corn, beans, peas, lentils, garbanzos (chickpeas) and *habas* (broad beans).

The *Criolla* (mission grape), was first planted at San Juan Capistrano in 1779. In 1783, the first wine produced in Alta California came from the mission's winery. The vineyards produced sacramental wine, a sweet dessert table wine called Angelica, and brandy in quantities sufficient for trade. Reports of the quality vary.

Tanned hides were also produced for trade. All the trade items were bartered for goods carried by the sailing ships, which stopped in San Juan Cove (now known as Dana Point Harbor).

The neophytes, who called themselves *Acjachemen*, were renamed *Juaneños* by the Spanish. They were hunter/gatherers at the time the Spanish arrived. In order to prepare them for the coming settlement and economy the Spanish anticipated, the Indians were taught skills like tanning, wine making, metalworking, and agriculture. The Franciscans intended for the mission and the lands to be given to the natives once they became self-sufficient. However, the Spanish were defeated by the Mexicans in 1821 before this plan could be executed.

In the years following the Mexican occupation, the missions were taxed. Many neophytes left the area, and even more died in a series of illnesses and plagues. Repeated cycles of drought and flood drove even more of the locals away from the area.

Mission Arches
11x14 oil on canvas

# Privatization

In 1846, Mexican Governor Pio Pico privatized the missions. Mission San Juan Capistrano was sold to Don Juan Forster, the governor's brother-in-law, for $760, far less than its actual value. The mission became the family's home for several years, even though they owned several other large ranchos nearby.

During the secularization period, most missions were stripped of their tiles and wooden beams to build houses. Unprotected adobe walls dissolved in the rain.

Mission San Juan fared a little better because Don Juan Forster actually lived in part of the mission and kept his trade goods stored in part of the Serra Chapel. However, his wife, a devout Catholic, insisted part of the chapel remain as a church. She provided a bed for any itinerant priest who was willing to conduct Mass. Therefore, the Serra Chapel is the only church built by Father Serra to be in constant use as a church from its construction to today.

During the Forsters' occupation, the adobe buildings used as their home and for storage were protected from the elements, but the north and west wings dissolved, leaving only their brick arches.

Old Arches
16x20 oil on canvas

# Los Rios Street

In 1794, forty adobe structures were constructed, many on what is presently called Los Rios Street (then called *Calle Occidental* or "West Street") to house the Indians who worked at the mission. The first of these was built by Feliciano Rios, a leather-jacket Spanish soldier married to a *Juaneño* native. Descendants of his family still occupy this home.

The Montañez Adobe is also believed to be one of the original structures. It was the home of Dona Polonia Montañez, the daughter of Tomas Gutierrez, an early mission carpenter. The Montañez Adobe gained spiritual significance following the secularization of the mission when Dona Montañez created a tiny chapel in the adobe where she educated the town's children. It became the village sanctuary during periods when the chapel wasn't available. She became the spiritual leader as well as the village midwife and nurse.

The city of San Juan Capistrano now owns and maintains this building. The Historical Society conducts guided tours of the building to teach local history. A butterfly garden welcomes visitors to the adobe.

The Los Rios Historical District, comprised of thirty structures, was listed on the National Register of Historic Places in 1983. Los Rios Street is the oldest continuously occupied street in the western United States.

Montañez Adobe
24x30 oil on canvas

Los Rios House SJC
11x14 oil on canvas

Ramos House Café
11x14 oil on canvas

Side Entrance – Cottage Gallery

16x20 oil on canvas

Pump House
24x36 oil on canvas

No Pumps Los Rios
11x14 oil on canvas

Aqua Trim-
11x14 oil on canvas

Hummingbird Cottage
11x14 oil on canvas

Mesa Home - Los Rios Street
9x12 oil on canvas

# The Bells

The four bells, which hung in the bell tower of the Great Stone Church, survived the earthquake. They were hung in a bell wall, or *campanario*, adjacent to the ruins of the church. The two largest bells are replicas.

Today, the original large bells hang in a location where the bell tower of the Great Stone Church once stood. The two smaller bells in the *campanario* are original.

The largest bell bears the inscription: "*Viva Jesus, Sn Vicente Advon De Los RRS PS Miros F VIcte Fustr IF JN SN TIAGO* 1796" The English Translation reads: "Praised be Jesus, San Vicente. In honor of the Rev. Fathers, Ministers (of the Mission) Fray Vicente Fuster, and Fray Juan Santiago, 1796." It is known as "San Vicente."

The next largest bell's inscription reads, "*ave maria purisima me fesit ruelas Ime yamo s. juan, 1796*" The English translation reads, "Hail Mary most pure. Ruelas made me, and my name is San Juan, 1796." It is called "San Juan."

The larger of the smaller two bells is inscribed: "*ave maria purisima, Sn Antonio, 1804.*" The English translation reads, "Hail Mary most pure, San Antonio, 1804." Its nickname is "San Antonio."

The smallest bell's inscription reads, "*Ave Maria Purisima San Rafael, 1804.*" The English translation reads, "Hail Mary most pure, San Rafael, 1804." It is known as "San Rafael."

Locally, ringing the bells is considered a great honor. The role of bell ringer is passed down through local families

Bells in Direct Light
11x14 oil on canvas

Dark Arch
11x14 oil on canvas

Gray Day Bells
16x20 oil on linen

Back of the Bells
16x20 oil on canvas

O'Sullivan's Garden
16x20 oil on canvas

Shadows Across the Bells
16x20 oil on canvas

**Silhouetted Bells**
30x40 oil on canvas

Moonlight Bells
11x14 oil on canvas

# The Depot

The current San Juan Capistrano train station is not the first to be built there. When the railroad link to San Juan was completed in 1887, the railroad constructed a one-story wooden structure with gables in the Queen Anne style. However, the local people did not like this building because it was not in keeping with their mission heritage.

The railroad agreed to build a new depot in the Mission Revival style. Completed in 1894, it is considered one of the most beautiful train stations in southern California.

In 1966, the station was closed, and in 1975, the depot was remodeled for use as a restaurant, incorporating some actual railroad cars in the design. The Amtrak ticket office is now located in one of these cars at the north end of the complex.

In the intervening years, several different restaurants have occupied the building and train cars. Its historic nature provides a lovely subject for artists and photographers.

The Depot SJC From Los Rios Street
16x20 oil on board

Welcome to Sarducci's
11x14 oil on canvas

Sarducci's Patio
9x12 oil on canvas

The Depot from Los Rios
11x14 oil on canvas

# The Jewel

Mission San Juan Capistrano originally received the nickname "The Jewel of the Missions" because of the Great Stone Church. Upon its completion in 1806 (following nine years of construction), it was considered a modern marvel and an architectural gem. No other church on the coast of California compared in size or beauty. Although the church did not survive the earthquake of 1812, its ruins still inspire visitors.

In 1865, the mission was returned to the Catholic Church by a decree signed by Abraham Lincoln. However, at the time, the church was in such a state of ruin the church authorities recommended it be torn down and sold. The town felt the mission deserved preservation because of its history.

The Landmarks Club, founded in Los Angeles in 1895, provided funds to begin the work. In 1910, Father John O'Sullivan became the resident priest. He led an effort to restore and rebuild the historic structure to a semblance of its earlier glory. San Juan then became a tourist destination. The Los Angeles art community arrived to make paintings and take photographs of the buildings, gardens, and fountains.

The spectacular gold altarpiece in the Serra Chapel, or *retablo*, was hand-carved in Barcelona from 396 individual pieces of cherry wood, overlaid in gold leaf. It is estimated to be 400 years old. It was originally imported in 1806 for the Los Angeles cathedral, but it was never used. It was installed at San Juan between 1922 and 1924. The roof of the north end of the building had to be raised to accommodate it. Extensive restoration was begun in June of 2006.

In the early years of the twentieth century, motion picture companies discovered the mission. Several early films were made there and drew additional attention to the location.

In 1984, a modern church, Mission Basilica San Juan Capistrano, was constructed to the north and west of the historic compound. Today, the old mission compound serves as a museum. The Serra Chapel still functions as a chapel for the mission parish.

Fountain Back Patio
11x14 oil on linen

Inner Courtyard
11x14 oil on canvas

Spring SJC Courtyard
16x20 oil on canvas

Mission Well
24x30 oil on canvas

Mission Reflections
11x14 oil on canvas

SJC Mission
11x14 oil on canvas

Mission and Pool
20x24 oil on linen

Bougainvillea
11x14 oil on canvas

From Pond to Junipero
11x14 oil on canvas

Inner Courtyard
11x14 oil on canvas

Altar – Serra Chapel
11x14 oil on canvas

Votive Candles Serra Chapel
11x14 oil on canvas

# The Legend of the Swallows

The American cliff swallow spends its winters in Argentina but makes the long trip north in the spring. According to legend, the birds have visited the San Juan Capistrano area every year for centuries, arriving on St. Joseph's Day, March nineteenth. According to the story, the birds first took refuge at the mission when an irate innkeeper destroyed their mud nests.

In 1915, an article in *Overland Monthly* magazine reported the birds' annual arrival at the mission. Father O'Sullivan capitalized on the public interest in the story to finance restoration.

A bell ringer, Acú, invented a fanciful addition in which the birds (*las golondrinas* in Spanish) flew across the Atlantic Ocean to Jerusalem each winter, carrying small twigs on which they landed on the water during their trip.

On March 19, 1936, a radio program was broadcast live from the Mission grounds, announcing the swallows' arrival. Composer Leon Rene was inspired by the event to pen the song "When the Swallows Come Back to Capistrano." Many famous artists, including The Ink Spots, Fred Waring, Guy Lombardo, Glenn Miller, and Pat Boone, recorded the song.

In recent years, fewer swallows return to the mission due to increased development. Many nesting places no longer exist, and fewer insects remain. Yet the celebration of the swallows continues.

Old Apse – Mission SJC
11x14 oil on canvas

Old Stone Sanctuary
11x14 oil on linen

# The Mission Today

In 1986, a modern church, Mission Basilica of San Juan Capistrano, was completed to the north and west of the historic compound. The new church, designed after the Old Stone Church, serves as the religious home for the parish. This facility not only hosts weekly Masses, but also serves as a community auditorium for concerts.

On the Feast of St. Joseph, March 19, 2003, the U.S. National Conference of Catholic Bishops designated Mission San Juan Capistrano as a National Shrine in recognition of the Mission's effective service to pilgrims from across the United States and the international community.

Today, the old mission compound serves as a museum. The Serra Chapel still functions as a chapel for the mission parish.

Mission SJC from Old San Juan Hill
8x10 oil on board

New Dome
11x14 oil on canvas

Docent
16x20 oil on canvas

Mission Visitors
11x14 oil on canvas

Visitors Mission SJC
11x14 oil on canvas

Carriage Ride
11x14 oil on canvas

# About the Author

**Lorna Collins** and her husband, Larry K. Collins, helped build the Universal Studios Japan theme park in Osaka Japan. Their memoir of that experience, ***31 Months in Japan: The Building of a Theme Park***, was published in 2005 and was an EPPIE finalist and chosen one of Rebeccas Reads best nonfiction books of 2005.

They have also co-written two cozy mysteries set in Hawaii: ***Murder…They Wrote*** and ***Murder in Paradise***, the latter a finalist for the EPIC eBook Award for mystery. They are currently working on more in the series.

Lorna co-authored six sweet romance anthologies set in the fictional town of Aspen Grove, CO: ***Snowflake Secrets, Seasons of Love, An Aspen Grove Christmas, The Art of Love***, ***…And a Silver Sixpence in Her Shoe***, and ***Directions of Love,*** 2011 EPIC eBook Award winner.

Her fantasy/mystery/romance, ***Ghost Writer***, set in Laguna Beach, CA, launched Oak Tree Press's Mystic Oaks imprint.

***The Memory Keeper,*** published in 2014, is Larry & Lorna's historical novel set in San Juan Capistrano in the 1800s. They are currently working on a sequel.

In addition, Lorna is a professional editor.

http://www.lornalarry.com

31months@cox.net

http://lornacollins-author.blogspot.com/

https://twitter.com/LornaCollins

# About the Artist

**Robert L. Schwenck** was born in Los Angeles and raised in Glendale. The beauty he observed around him inspired Bob to attempt to capture it at an early age. He received a National Art Association Scholarship and earned his Bachelor of Arts degree in Drawing and Painting from UCLA. But the ministry beckoned, and he went on to earn his Masters of Divinity from Princeton Seminary. During his thirty-seven years in the ministry (over thirty years serving the Community Presbyterian Church of San Juan Capistrano where he is now Pastor Emeritus), he continued to marvel at the beauty he saw in the world.

Bob Schwenck paints with clarity, strength and vitality. He uses saturated color and vigorous brushstrokes to communicate the creation's spiritual foundations.

In recent years, he has had several one-man shows in Southern California including showing his work at Mission San Juan Capistrano and several private showings. He has done numerous commissions, working both from photographs and live subjects and has had his work displayed in local galleries in San Juan Capistrano and Dana Point. He has served on the staff at Ghost Ranch in New Mexico teaching painting.

He is one of the featured artists in the book *Art of the American West* by Caroline Linscott and Julie Christiansen-Dull, a collection of the best work of contemporary western artists. His recent book, *Innerscape,* includes images of his latest introspective work.

Robert L. Schwenck's work is displayed at The Cottage Gallery on Los Rios in San Juan Capistrano. Please stop by and see his paintings along with those of other exceptionally talented local artists.

Robert Schwenck is an award-winning member of San Clemente Art Association and can be seen in shows throughout Southern California. Now, happily retired, Bob Schwenck resides—and paints—in Dana Point, California with occasional trips to other locales in search of his next inspiration.

# About the Artwork

The paintings included in this book are all the work of Robert L. Schwenck. Some have been sold, but most are still available for purchase. Please contact the artist at schwenckart@cox.net to inquire about purchasing these and other works by the artist.

http://www.schwenckart.com

schwenckart@cox.net

Made in the USA
Las Vegas, NV
03 March 2021

19013554R10052